Trivial Matters for Children

101 Lists for Memorization

By Mark Foley

978-0-6151-9609-1

For Kate and Maxim

You remember the tiniest details—this book seemed only natural.

Introduction

You may be wondering why knowing the names of the noble gases is so important. Or you may be asking yourself, "Why does my 8-year-old daughter need to know that Miles Davis and Ella Fitzgerald are two famous jazz musicians?" The answer to question number one is: Ultimately it is not. Number two? She really doesn't. But I would argue that the mere act of memorizing lists like this is an activity that will enrich a child's learning and build a framework for future lessons.

Memorization is an activity that gets a bad rap, but one that can be a very useful tool. As a physician I hear a lot of things. "Medical school—I bet that was tough." Or, "Is being a doctor hard?" I usually tell people that if they can memorize they can become a doctor. Don't get me wrong, there is no way that knowing the Seven Modern Wonders of the World is *really* going to help a surgeon locate the appendix, but training my mind to memorize lists of information at an early age helped me develop the ability to retain facts that can later be put into proper context, whether that be caring for sick patients or repairing my children's computer. Rote memorization as "busy work" or as a substitution for learning is ill-advised. Memorization as a tool to build "brain power" can be useful and fun.

This book started as a way to have our daughter memorize a few lists in order to expose her to concepts we would later teach her in our homeschooling. We kept track of the lists she memorized and then gave her a prize for every five lists she "passed off." Given her incredible love of reading, the prize was usually a trip to the bookstore to pick out a new book. One of our friends saw our book and said she'd love to have a little book with a bunch of lists so she could toss it in her purse and homeschool "on the go." So I decided to add to the number of lists until I had one hundred. Then I added one more because "101 Lists for Memorization" had a certain ring to it.

I've divided the lists into sections for easier digestion, all the while keeping in mind the variety of ages for which this book is intended. While I'd expect late elementary school-aged children to be able to rattle off the names of the chess pieces, I might save a list of Shakespeare's tragedies for a child who is a little older. Remember, however, that children will surprise you with their ability to memorize seemingly difficult lists. I've divided lengthy lists (for example, state capitals or U.S. presidents) into multiple lists of ten or so items and I've even thrown in a few original poems, just to "change things up." As for the lists of great musicians, artists, philosophers, *etc.*—I chose the ones *I* readily think of, not the *actual* Ten Greatest Philosophers. We all know our opinions vary, but I think these lists of "greats" are worthwhile whatever your thoughts on the subject.

Hopefully you will find enjoyment in memorizing with your children or the children you teach, and you will most certainly be surprised at their capacity to retain seemingly complex information. More than anything I hope these lists can be a way to initiate discussions and learning about world religions, art, music, technology, politics, and any other range of topics that will broaden the minds of our children.

Contents

Everyday Things

Colors of the Rainbow

Red

Orange

Yellow

Green

Blue

Violet

Days of the Week

Sunday

Monday

Tuesday

Wednesday

Thursday

Friday

Saturday

Seasons

Spring

Summer

Autumn/Fall

Winter

Months of the Year

January

February

March

April

May

June

July

August

September

October

November

December

U.S. Coins

Penny

Nickel

Dime

Quarter

Half-dollar

Dollar

U.S. Currency (Bills)

1

2

5

10

20

50

100

Directions

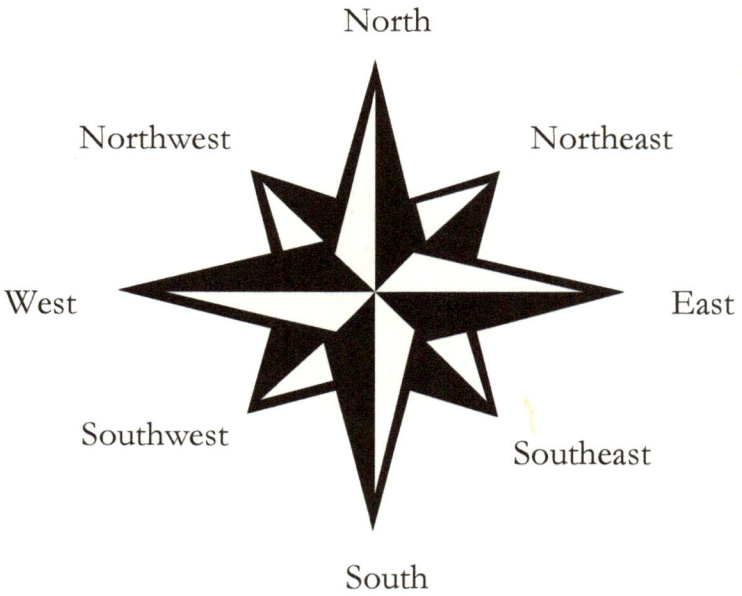

North

Northwest

Northeast

West

East

Southwest

Southeast

South

U.S. Time Zones

Eastern

Central

Mountain

Pacific

Hawaii

Alaska

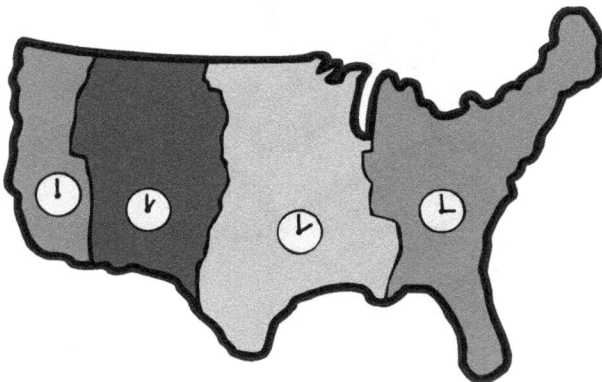

Home Keys on a Keyboard

A S D F G H J K L ;

Science

Planets

Mercury

Venus

Earth

Mars

Jupiter

Saturn

Uranus

Neptune

Pluto

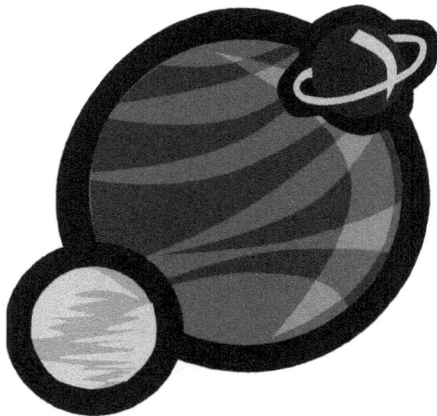

Systems of the Body

Circulatory

Digestive

Endocrine

Integumentary

Muscular

Nervous

Reproductive

Respiratory

Skeletal

Urinary

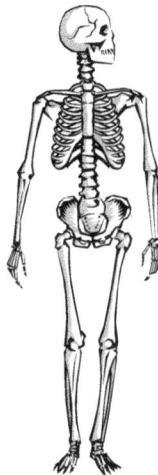

Organs of the Body

Brain

Heart

Lungs

Stomach

Intestines

Liver

Kidney

Muscle

Bone

Skin

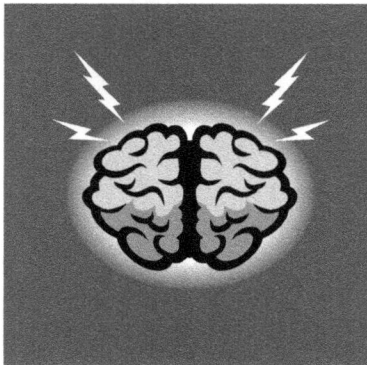

Eight Great Inventors

Alexander Graham Bell (Telephone)

Wilbur and Orville Wright (Airplane)

Thomas Edison (Light Bulb)

Eli Whitney (Cotton Gin)

Benjamin Franklin (Bifocal Glasses)

Samuel Morse (Telegraph)

Louis Braille (Braille Writing)

Isaac Singer (Sewing Machine)

Metric Units of Measure

Millimeter (mm)

Centimeter (cm)

Meter (m)

Kilometer (km)

Milligram (mg)

Gram (g)

Kilogram (kg)

Milliliter (mL)

Liter (L)

Noble Gases

(Chemistry)

Helium (He)

Neon (Ne)

Argon (Ar)

Krypton (Kr)

Xenon (Xe)

Radon (Ra)

Ununoctium (Uuo)

Electromagnetic Spectrum

Radio

Microwave

Infrared

Visible Light

Ultraviolet

X-ray

Gamma Ray

Geologic Eras

Precambrian

Palaeozoic

Mesozoic

Cainozoic

Most Common Elements on Earth

Oxygen (O)

Silicon (Si)

Aluminum (Al)

Iron (Fe)

Calcium (Ca)

Sodium (Na)

Potassium (K)

Magnesium (Mg)

Fun Stuff

The Seven Dwarves

Doc

Happy

Sneezy

Sleepy

Grumpy

Bashful

Dopey

Chess Pieces

King

Queen

Bishop

Knight

Rook

Pawn

Pixar Movies

(Through 2007)

Toy Story

Toy Story 2

Monsters, Inc.

A Bug's Life

Finding Nemo

The Incredibles

Cars

Ratatouille

Decathlon Events

100 meters

Long Jump

Shot Put

High Jump

400 meters

110 meter Hurdles

Discus Throwing

Pole Vault

Javelin Throwing

1500 meters

Golf Clubs

Driver

Woods

Irons

Pitching Wedge

Sand Wedge

Putter

(Extra Credit: Hybrids)

Baseball

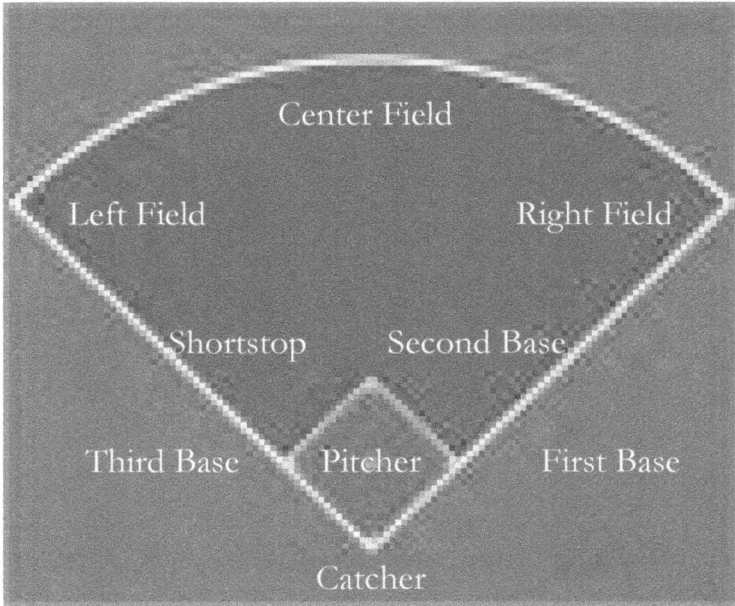

Center Field

Left Field   Right Field

Shortstop   Second Base

Third Base   Pitcher   First Base

Catcher

Ball

Strike

Out

Run

Hit

Error

Music

Mozart

Musical Notes

Do

Re

Mi

Fa

So

La

Ti

Do

Orchestra Sections

Strings

Woodwinds

Brass

Percussion

Instruments of the Orchestra

Violin

Viola

Cello

Bass

Piccolo

Flute

Oboe

Clarinet

Bassoon

Trumpet

French Horn

Trombone

Tuba

Percussion

Flats (Music)

Bb

Eb

Ab

Db

Gb

Cb

Fb

Sharps (Music)

F#

C#

G#

D#

A#

E#

B#

Modes of the Major Scale

Ionian

Dorian

Phrygian

Lydian

Mixolydian

Aeolian

Locrian

(Ionian)

Woodwind Instruments

Flute

Clarinet

Saxophone

Oboe

Bassoon

Bagpipes

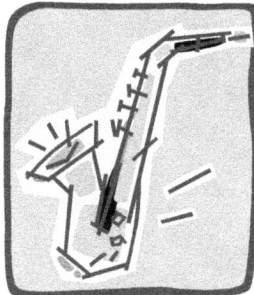

Brass Instruments

Baritone

Bugle

Cornet

Trumpet

Trombone

Tuba

Sousaphone

String Instruments

Violin

Viola

Cello

Bass

Harp

Banjo

Guitar

Percussion Instruments

Bass Drum

Bells

Castanets

Chimes

Cymbals

Piano

Snare Drum

Timpani

Tom-Tom

Xylophone

Notes on the Keyboard

	C
	B
Bb/A#	
	A
Ab/G#	
	G
Gb/F#	
	F
	E
Eb/D#	
	D
Db/C#	
	C

Ten Great Composers

Johann Sebastian Bach

Ludwig van Beethoven

Johannes Brahms

Frederic Chopin

George Frederic Handel

Franz Joseph Haydn

Gustav Holst

Felix Mendelssohn

Wolfgang Amadeus Mozart

Piotr Ilyitch Tchaikovsky

Beethoven

Jazz Music Genres

Dixieland

Big Band

Swing

Bebop

Fusion

Avant-Garde

Vocal

Progressive

Crossover

Ten Great Jazz Musicians

Louis Armstrong

Count Basie

John Coltrane

Miles Davis

Duke Ellington

Ella Fitzgerald

Benny Goodman

J.J. Johnson

Wynton Marsalis

Charlie Parker

Art, Literature, and Mythology

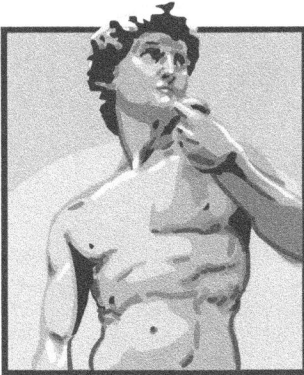

Greek (Olympian) Gods

Zeus	(sky)
Poseiden	(waters)
Hades	(underworld)
Hestia	(hearth)
Hera	(marriage, childbirth)
Aris	(war)
Athena	(reason, intelligence, art, wisdom)
Apollo	(music)
Aphrodite	(love, beauty)
Hermes	(messenger)
Artemis	(nature)
Hephaestus	(fire)

Roman Gods

(With Greek Counterparts)

Jupiter	(Zeus)
Neptune	(Poseiden)
Pluto	(Hades)
Vesta	(Hestia)
Juno	(Hera)
Mars	(Aris)
Minerva	(Athena)
Apollo	(Apollo)
Venus	(Aphrodite)
Mercury	(Hermes)
Diana	(Artemis)
Vulcan and Mulciber	(Hephaestus)

Shakespeare's Comedies

All's Well That Ends Well

As You Like It

The Comedy of Errors

Cymbeline

Love's Labours Lost

Measure for Measure

The Merry Wives of Windsor

The Merchant of Venice

A Midsummer Night's Dream

Much Ado About Nothing

Pericles, Prince of Tyre

Taming of the Shrew

The Tempest

Troilus and Cressida

Twelfth Night

Two Gentlemen of Verona

Winter's Tale

Shakespeare's Tragedies

Antony and Cleopatra

Coriolanus

Hamlet

Julius Caesar

King Lear

Macbeth

Othello

Romeo and Juliet

Timon of Athens

Titus Andronicus

Three (Four) Musketeers

Aramis

Athos

Porthos

D'Artagnan

Ten Great Philosophers

Socrates

Plato

Aristotle

St. Thomas Aquinas

Niccolò Machiavelli

René Descartes

John Locke

Immanuel Kant

Georg Hegel

Friedrich Nietzsche

Harry Potter Novels

By J.K. Rowling

The Sorcerer's Stone*

The Chamber of Secrets

The Prisoner of Azkaban

The Goblet of Fire

The Order of the Phoenix

The Half-Blood Prince

The Deathly Hallows

*The U.K. title of Book 1 is *The Philosopher's Stone*

Ten Great Artists

Michelangelo Buonarroti

Mary Cassat

Salvador Dali

Leonardo DaVinci

Claude Monet

Pablo Picasso

Pierre-Auguset Renoir

Rembrandt van Rijn

Vincent Van Gogh

Andy Warhol

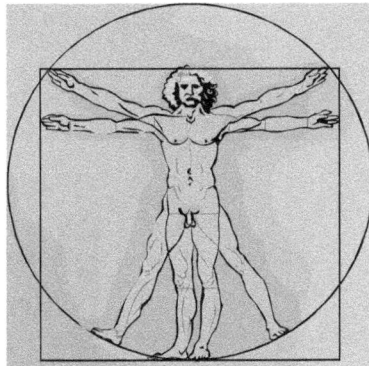

World Facts
(Geography and Other Stuff)

Continents

Africa

Antarctica

Asia

Australia

Europe

North America

South America

Oceans of the World

Arctic

Atlantic

Indian

Pacific

Southern

Seven Wonders of the Ancient World

Pyramid at Giza

Hanging Gardens of Babylon

Temple of Artemis at Ephesus

Statute of Zeus at Olympia

Mausoleum of Maussolos at Halicarnassus

Colossus of Rhodes

Lighthouse of Alexandria

Seven Wonders of the Modern World

(From the American Society of Civil Engineers)

Empire State Building

Itaipu Dam

CN Tower

Panama Canal

Channel Tunnel

North Sea Protection Works

Golden Gate Bridge

Ten Famous Explorers

Christopher Columbus

Vasco da Gama

Ferdinand Magellan

Roald Amundsen

Lewis and Clark

Jacques Cartier

Leif Ericsson

Ponce de Leon

Sir Francis Drake

Edmund Hillary

Columbus

Five Longest Rivers

(World)

Nile

Amazon

Yangtze

Hwang Ho

Congo

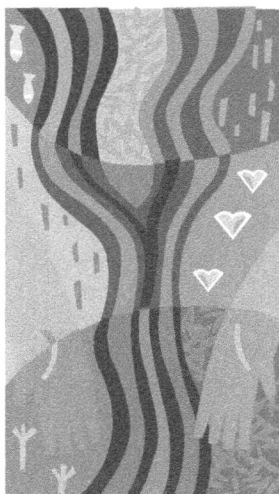

Eight Largest Countries in the World

Russia

Canada

United States

China

Brazil

Australia

India

Argentina

Ten Most Populated Countries

China

India

United States

Indonesia

Brazil

Pakistan

Russia

Bangladesh

Japan

Nigeria

United Nations
Permanent Security Council Members

The United States

The United Kingdom (Great Britain)

The Russian Federation

France

China

The Big Three

(Yalta Conference—World War II)

Winston Churchill (U.K.)

Franklin D. Roosevelt (U.S.)

Joseph Stalin (U.S.S.R.)

Roosevelt

Provinces and Territories of Canada

Ontario

Quebec

Nova Scotia

New Brunswick

Manitoba

British Columbia

Prince Edward Island

Saskatchewan

Alberta

Newfoundland and Labrador

Northwest Territories

Yukon

Nunavut

The United States
(Geography, Politics, and Other Facts)

State Capitals, Part 1

Alabama	Montgomery
Alaska	Juneau
Arkansas	Little Rock
Arizona	Phoenix
California	Sacramento
Colorado	Denver
Connecticut	Hartford
Delaware	Dover
Florida	Tallahassee
Georgia	Atlanta

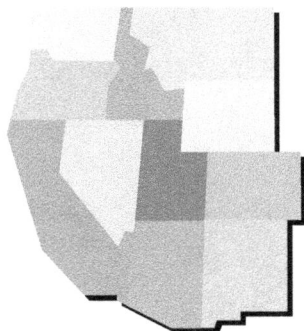

State Capitals, Part 2

Hawaii	Honolulu
Idaho	Boise
Illinois	Springfield
Indiana	Indianapolis
Iowa	Des Moines
Kansas	Topeka
Kentucky	Frankfort
Louisiana	Baton Rouge
Maine	Augusta
Maryland	Annapolis

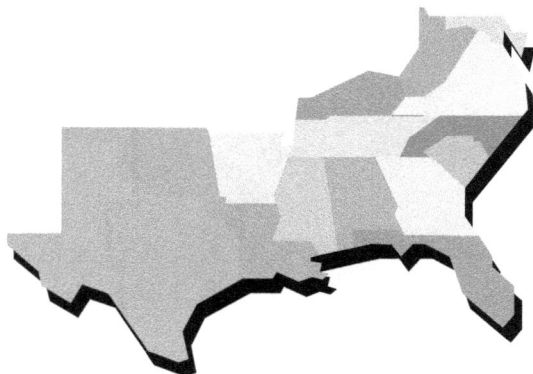

State Capitals, Part 3

Massachusetts	Boston
Michigan	Lansing
Minnesota	St. Paul
Mississippi	Jackson
Missouri	Jefferson City
Montana	Helena
Nebraska	Lincoln
Nevada	Carson City
New Hampshire	Concord
New Jersey	Trenton

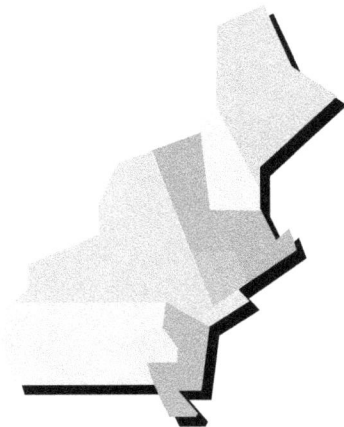

State Capitals, Part 4

New Mexico	Santa Fe
New York	Albany
North Carolina	Raleigh
North Dakota	Bismarck
Ohio	Columbus
Oklahoma	Oklahoma City
Oregon	Salem
Pennsylvania	Harrisburg
Rhode Island	Providence
South Carolina	Columbia

State Capitals, Part 5

South Dakota	Pierre
Tennessee	Nashville
Texas	Austin
Utah	Salt Lake City
Vermont	Montpelier
Virginia	Richmond
Washington	Olympia
West Virginia	Charleston
Wisconsin	Madison
Wyoming	Cheyenne

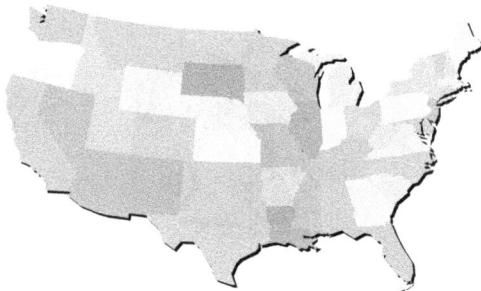

Original U.S. Colonies

Connecticut

Delaware

Georgia

Maryland

Massachusetts

New Hampshire

New Jersey

New York

North Carolina

Pennsylvania

Rhode Island

South Carolina

Virginia

Branches of Government

(United States)

Executive (President)

Legislative (Congress)

Judicial (Supreme Court)

Five Longest Rivers

(United States)

Missouri

Mississippi

Yukon

Rio Grande

St. Lawrence

Ten Largest States in the U.S.

Alaska

Texas

California

Montana

New Mexico

Arizona

Nevada

Colorado

Oregon

Wyoming

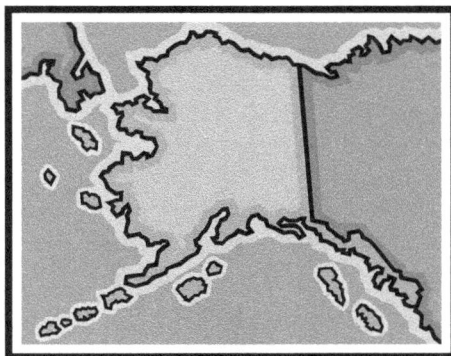

Confederate States

South Carolina

Mississippi

Florida

Alabama

Georgia

Louisiana

Texas

Virginia

Arkansas

North Carolina

Tennessee

First Amendment Rights

Speech

Press

Assembly

Religion

Petition

Supreme Court Justices, 2008

John G. Roberts (Chief)

John Paul Stevens

Antonin Scalia

Anthony M. Kennedy

David Hackett Souter

Clarence Thomas

Ruth Bader Ginsburg

Stephen G. Breyer

Samuel Anthony Alito, Jr.

Apollo 11 Crew

(First Lunar Landing—July 20, 1969)

Neil Armstrong

Michael Collins

Edwin "Buzz" Aldrin

Top U.S. Newspapers

(2007 Circulation)

USA Today

Wall Street Journal

New York Times

Los Angeles Times

Chicago Tribune

Inalienable Rights

(Declaration of Independence)

Life

Liberty

Pursuit of Happiness

Wars of the United States

(Through the 20th Century)

American Revolution

The War of 1812

Mexican-American War

World War I

World War II

Korean War

Vietnam War

Desert Storm

Monuments in Washington, D.C.

Marine Corps (Iwo Jima) War Memorial

Jefferson Memorial

Korean War Veterans Memorial

World War II Memorial

Tomb of the Unknown Soldier

Vietnam Veterans' Memorial

Washington Monument

Ten Most Populated Cities

(United States)

New York

Los Angeles

Chicago

Houston

Philadelphia

Phoenix

San Diego

Dallas

San Antonio

Detroit

Presidents of the United States, Part 1

Washington George

John Adams

Thomas Jefferson

James Madison

James Monroe

John Quincy Adams

Andrew Jackson

Martin Van Buren

William Harrison

John Tyler

James Polk

Washington

Presidents of the United States, Part 2

Zachary Taylor

Millard Fillmore

Franklin Pierce

James Buchanan

Abraham Lincoln

Andrew Johnson

Ulysses S. Grant

Rutherford Hayes

James Garfield

Chester Arthur

Grover Cleveland

Lincoln

Presidents of the United States, Part 3

Benjamin Harrison

Grover Cleveland

William McKinley

Theodore Roosevelt

William Taft

Woodrow Wilson

Warren Harding

Calvin Coolidge

Herbert Hoover

Franklin D. Roosevelt

Harry Truman

Presidents of the United States, Part 4

Dwight D. Eisenhower

John F. Kennedy

Lyndon B. Johnson

Richard Nixon

Gerald Ford

Jimmy Carter

Ronald Reagan

George Bush

Bill Clinton

George W. Bush

Kennedy

Religion

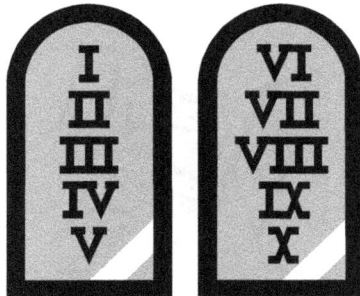

Books of the Torah

Genesis

Exodus

Leviticus

Numbers

Deuteronomy

The Twelve Tribes of Israel

Asher

Benjamin

Dan

Gad

Issachar

Joseph

(Ephraim)

(Manasseh)

Judah

Levi

Naphtali

Reuben

Simeon

Zebulon

Three Wise Men and Their Gifts
(Western Tradition)

Caspar

Melchior

Balthazar

Gold

Frankincense

Myrrh

Ten Commandments

Thou shalt have no other gods before me

Thou shalt not worship idols

Thou shalt not take the name of God in vain

Remember the Sabbath day, to keep it holy

Honor thy father and thy mother

Thou shalt not kill

Thou shalt not commit adultery

Thou shalt not steal

Thou shalt not lie

Thou shalt not covet

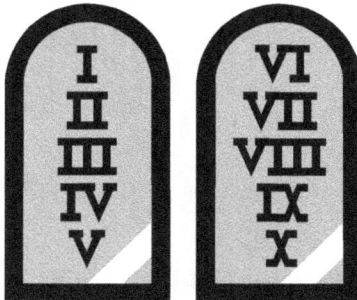

Pillars of Islam

Testimony of Faith (Shahadah)

Ritual Prayer (Salat)

Obligatory Almsgiving (Zakat)

Fasting (Sawm)

The Pilgrimage to Mecca (Hajj)

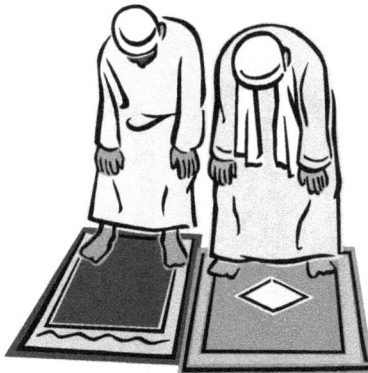

The Gospels

(New Testament)

Matthew

Mark

Luke

John

Parts of Speech

Noun

Verb

Pronoun

Adjective

Adverb

Conjunction

Interjection

Punctuation Marks

Period (.)

Comma (,)

Quotation Mark (")

Apostrophe (')

Colon (:)

Semicolon (;)

Hyphen (-)

Exclamation Point (!)

Question Mark (?)

Parentheses ( )

Counting to Ten

(Spanish)

Uno

Dos

Tres

Cuatro

Cinco

Seis

Siete

Ocho

Nueve

Diez

Counting to Ten

(French)

Un

Deux

Trois

Quatre

Cinq

Six

Sept

Huit

Neuf

Dix

Counting to Ten

(German)

Eins

Zwei

Drei

Vier

Fünf

Sechs

Sieben

Acht

Neun

Zehn

Counting to Ten

(Japanese)

Ichi

Ni

San

Shi

Go

Roku

Shichi

Hachi

Kyu

Ju

Greek Alphabet

Alpha (A, α)
Beta (B, β)
Gamma(Γ, γ)
Delta (Δ, δ)
Epsilon (E, ε)
Zeta (Z, ζ)
Eta (H, η)
Theta (Θ, θ)
Iota (I, ι)
Kappa (K, κ)
Lambda (Λ, λ)
Mu (M, μ)
Nu (N, ν)
Xi (Ξ, ξ)
Omicron (O, o)
Pi (Π, π)
Rho (P, ϱ)
Sigma (Σ, σ)
Tau (T, τ)
Upsilon (Υ, υ)
Phi (Φ, φ)
Chi (X, χ)
Psi (Ψ, ψ)
Omega (Ω, ω)

Silly Poetry

by Mark Foley

Australia

Crocodiles and dingoes

And wild kangaroos,

Koalas, aborigines,

And didgeridoos.

Where cookies are biscuits

And crackers are, too.

Things are very different there,

But the people . . .

They're just like me and you.

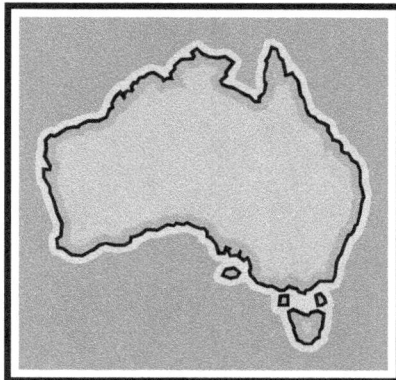

The Man from Bombay

There once was a man from Bombay
Who had something important to say.
"If you aren't in a hurry
You can eat some great curry
And then you can be on your way."

Bored Monkey

There once was this monkey in the zoo

Who never knew quite what to do.

So he climbed up a tree

And stared right at me.

So I just sat down and stared, too.

Random Things

Directions in a Boat

Fore

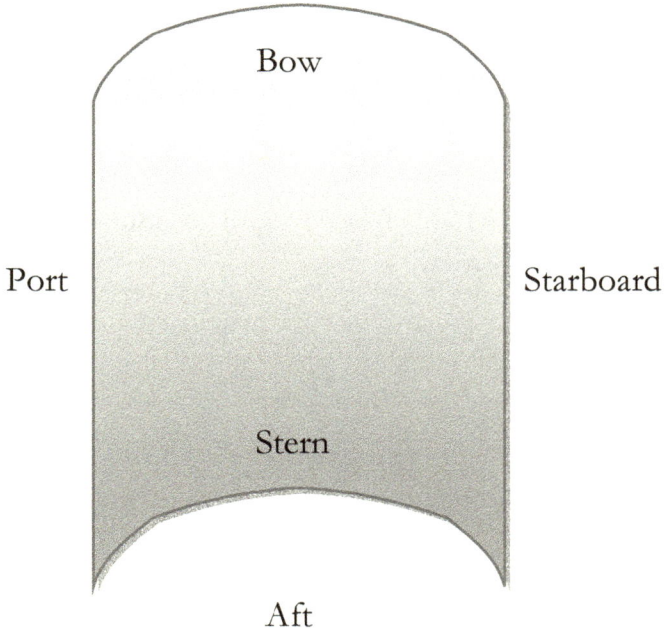

Bow

Port   Starboard

Stern

Aft

Birthstones

January	Garnet
February	Amethyst
March	Aquamarine
April	Diamond
May	Emerald
June	Pearl
July	Ruby
August	Peridot
September	Sapphire
October	Opal
November	Topaz
December	Turquoise

Five Quotes from Poor Richard

A word to the wise is enough.

God helps them that help themselves.

But dost thou love life? Then do not squander time,

for that's the stuff life is made of.

Early to bed and early to rise, makes a man healthy,

wealthy and wise.

A penny saved is a penny earned.

Ivy League Universities

Brown University

Columbia University

Cornell University

Dartmouth College

Harvard University

Princeton University

University of Pennsylvania

Yale University

Signs of the Zodiac

Aires

Taurus

Gemini

Cancer

Leo

Virgo

Libra

Scorpio

Sagittarius

Capricorn

Aquarius

Pisces

PISCES

Chinese Animal Zodiac

Rat

Ox

Tiger

Rabbit

Dragon

Snake

Horse

Sheep

Monkey

Rooster

Dog

Boar/Pig

www.ingramcontent.com/pod-product-compliance
Lightning Source LLC
Chambersburg PA
CBHW022306060426
42446CB00007BA/635